Volla Volla Jew Boy

Cyril Spector

Centerprise Publishing Project

Published by Centerprise Trust Ltd,
136 Kingsland High Street, Hackney E8 2NS
Typeset, Layout and Printed by
Lithosphere Printing Co-operative Ltd,
203/205 Pentonville Rd, London N1 9NF.

Centerprise is grateful for funding from Greater London Arts
Association, Inner London Education Authority and London
Borough of Hackney

1SBN 090373871 6

Contents

For my children
Jonathan, Adam and Felicity

Introduction

by Dr David Cesarani

The Jews of Britain are commonly held up as an example of how an immigrant group can rapidly establish itself and prosper in a new home, but is this interpretation entirely correct? Cyril Spector's recollections of Jewish life in East London between the wars are a salutory reminder that it was not a straight line from the immigrant ships of the 1880s-1900s to the Cabinet in the 1980s. His memoirs give a sharp, moving insight into the economic struggles of the East European Jews who settled in London and the difficulties faced by their children born or brought up as British subjects. Through his story it is possible to learn of the emotional and cultural cost of migration to a strange and not wholly receptive country — the loss of traditions and the estrangement between parents from one world and children brought up in another. Anglo-Jewry has, indeed, made remarkable strides from the slums of the East End; but the myth of success needs to be questioned and Cyril Spector reminds us of the too-often forgotten decades of toil and hardship before the Second World War.

When Cyril Spector was born in 1921, the Jewish community of East London was already much changed from the days of mass immigration. The Aliens Act of 1905 — Britain's first immigration legislation, directed primarily against the Jews — had virtually cut off the influx of Jews from Eastern Europe; by the 1920s, two thirds of East London Jews were British-born. Although the largest proportion of Jews was still to be found in Stepney — which embraced most of the first area of settlement, particularly Whitechapel — there has been a steady migration outwards to Hackney and Stoke Newington. Nevertheless, there were still around 100-150,000 Jews in the East End of London and adjacent districts, making it one of the greatest concentration of immigrants and their descendents in the whole of Britain.

The occupational profile of the Jews had shifted along with their residential pattern. For the immigrant generation, the chief sources of livelihood were tailoring, boot and shoe making and cabinet-making. The Census of 1901 showed that 40% of employed Jews were in the clothing trades, 12% in the manufacture of footwear and 10% in furniture production. Thirty years later, due to mechanisation, tailoring absorbed half as many Jews seeking work as it had done. Few Jews now worked in the boot and shoe industry which was also a casualty of competition from mass production.

Of the old immigrant trades, only cabinet-making prospered into the late 1920s, and even then its resilience was precarious. As Cyril Spector's memoir shows, economic fluctuations could fling an independent 'master', working in partnership with family or friends, back into the ranks of the workers. Success was tenuous and often fleeting. The small-scale cabinet makers had to compete with machine production, a war of attrition which the old artisan was doomed to lose. It is interesting that several other inter-war Jewish memoirs are set against this background. 'Volla Volla Jewboy' will join Harry Blacker's 'Just Like It Was. Memoirs of the Mittel East' and Ralph Glasser's 'Growing Up in the Gorbals' as a testimony to the grinding labour of the Jewish furniture trades.

Cyril, his brother and sister found work that was highly typical of the inter-war generation. His brother went into the new, mechanised furniture factories; his sister worked in a clothes shop. Cyril acquired an unskilled white-collar job after failing miserably as a carpenter. A small number of gifted East End Jewish kids made it into the professions, but most never had the chance to get into the right kind of school, to stay there long enough or ever afford university. Even if they got a good education and qualifications they faced discrimination in many sectors of employment — including the Civil Service, which would not employ people who were born outside of Britain. As a consequence, Jews bunched together in a narrow range of jobs. Many, like Cyril, found low-skilled clerical employment. Large numbers also gravitated towards the retail and distributive trades (everything from shop assistants and working the markets to travelling salesmen) taxi driving and hairdressing. Before and even after the Second World War, these were known as characteristically 'Jewish' occupations in much the same way as is the case for accountancy today.

Poor employment opportunities and low income went hand in hand. When the Spector household was hit by the slump, they were forced to move and share a house with another family. This house had no bath or indoor toilet. This was common in East

London: on the eve of World War Two, only 6% of working class dwellings in the borough of Stepney could boast an indoor lavatory and things were not much different in Bethnal Green, Shoreditch or many parts of Hackney. Cyril's brother and sister lived at home and for part of his youth, like thousands of East End children, he shared a bed with another member of the family. Home life was noisy and crowded.

Of course, the home was also a place of familiarity and comfort. In a Jewish household, children could look forward to the annual round of festivals, each with its particular culinary delights imported from the old country. Yet the force of religion was waning and young British-born and educated Jews were growing distant from their Yiddish-speaking parents who didn't 'fit in' so well to British society. Along with thousands of immigrants, Cyril's father read 'Di Tsait' — the Yiddish daily which mixed lurid crime stories with news of the 'old country' and events in England. Together, Cyril and his father visited the Yiddish theatre. At home, his parents spoke Yiddish, the 'mame loshn' — the mother-tongue of Jews in Eastern Europe. They were uneasy in British society, and for a long time, were fearful of involvement in British politics. Until he was naturalised Mr Spector, from Ekaterinoslav, could indeed have been deported for engaging in 'subversive' political activity and it is, therefore, no surprise that he avoided involvement in zionism or socialism. To the more self-confident British-born generation, their parents seemed passive and hapless victims of circumstances.

Novels of the East End from the 1930s, like Simon Blumenfeld's 'Jew Boy' and Willie Goldman's 'East End My Cradle' tell the story of this second-generation, strung out between a culture that had lost its meaning for them and a society that refused to accept them as equals. Visits to the synagogue and religious education were rituals performed largely to please parents: in themselves they meant less and less. Yiddish was discouraged by Jewish youth cubs and frowned upon in all mainstream communal organisations: the ideal was to turn young Jews into good British citizens. This was achieved, but at the cost of estrangement from a rich Yiddish cultural tradition and the decline of Jewish learning in general. There were no local authorities to patronise mother-tongue education or to put on multi-cultural events.

Despite this acculturation, Jews still faced discrimination and anti-semitism. Young Cyril had to be taken away from one school because of anti-Jewish bullying and he found Fascist sympathisers at Hackney Downs School. As the 'thirties went by, he became aware of political currents in Europe and in Britain, in particular the advance of Fascist and racist political movements. The East End was a battleground between rival ideologies — Zionism, Socialism, Communism, Fascism. Dalston was a stronghold of the British Union of Fascists and Ridley Road was on the front line. Throughout the '30s, East London saw frequently violent clashes between the left and Mosley's Blackshirts, culminating (but not ending) with the 'Battle of Cable Street' in October 1936. In the eyes of many young Jews, the Communists were the only political party to take the threat of Fascism seriously and its ranks were filled with angry Jews looking for a way to fight back and also to improve the life of East London's population, Jews and non-Jews alike. While he didn't join the CP, Cyril was drawn to it until the shock of Stalin's pact with Hitler in 1939 disillusioned him. Again, his experience was typical of thousands of Jewish East Londoners between the Wars.

In these years, a Jewish ethnic identity was forged that survived the war and was transplanted to the new Jewish surburban communities in North West, North and North East London. For some Jews it was built around religious ritual and the sense of community set apart from other people. For others it was founded upon Jewish social organisations like friendly societies or political activity such as Zionism or the labour movement. Networks of family, friendship and neighbourhood spirit helped these Jewish enclaves to cohere and reproduce themselves. For the third generation, the memory of immigration and settlement has, itself, become a part of contemporary Jewish identity. Yet this memory is frequently romanticised and distorted, to the detriment of a correct understanding of the Anglo-Jewish heritage and a sympathetic understanding of the experience of immigrants in the post-World War II era. While there are huge differences between the saga of Jews and that of immigrants from the Commonwealth and Pakistan, there are also similarities that are obscured if the myth of success is repeated unceasingly and uncritically.

Cyril Spector has bestowed a great favour on all sections of London's multi-ethnic population today. He offers to Jews and non Jews an insight into the experience of the Jewish immigrant and second-generation, with all its toil, troubles and personal tragedies. His story should warn us to be wary of the simplistic myth of Jewish immigrant success and to be more sensitive to the dislocations which afflicted the immigrants and their children. By extension, this should encourage a better appreciation of what later waves of immigrants have gone through — and what they are still experiencing, many of them in the very streets and districts once populated by Jews.

Dr David Cesarani is a Senior Research Fellow and Lecturer in Politics at Queen Mary College, University of London.

Preface

Standing at the edge of the Columbia Road Flower Market in 1984, I gazed over a large housing development to the area where I had been born and realised that the house and the road where I had lived was gone. So was the life and culture of my childhood. I felt I should recall my childhood to my children, so that it should never be forgotten. I had deeply resented not knowing anything about my parents' early days and so I was resolved that Jonathan, Adam and Felicity should get a brief picture of what it was like for their father growing up in Bethnal Green and Hackney. The thirty and forty years that separate our childhoods are a world apart and my world is almost forgotten, so remote it must seem to them.

So I recorded this as a personal narrative, intending it only for their eyes and for my wife, Renee, who grew up a few years later so near to where much of this is recorded.

1 Formative Years

What are the important aspects of the first memories of life? Why are these apparently trivial ones impressed on the memory when so many other and more important events and impressions are lost for ever? What does the psycho-analyst do in dragging up the hidden past in order to discover the reasons for present behaviour? He would have to start with my first memory, when I was about two years old, and try to make something out of that.

I could not have been more than two years old at the time and this first precious memory I can recall was of being dried by my mother after a bath. I was standing on a table in our front room, the tin bath was on a stool in front of me and I was gazing out on to the street. All I could see were the grey pavements and a large grey brick wall in front of me. Grey seemed to be a predominant colour in my childhood. This was the house that I was born in and lived in for the first three years of my life. I have only a few vague memories of this tiny house, with its small back yard and steep steps, situated in a narrow road off Brick Lane in the heart of the Jewish quarter of Bethnal Green. The house, and indeed Chambord Street itself, have long since gone and with it the bustling gregarious Jewish community that lived and worked there.

I was an unwanted child, a mistake, if ever there was one, and the scars remain to this day. My mother had never intended to have another child, she was in her mid-forties, so I can well imagine the consternation and concern that must have taken place when she discovered she was pregnant. Just as well that I wasn't around as I might have decided not to come! Still, in 1921 Jews did not discuss abortion and there was no reason why my mother should not deliver this child. I was the fifth child in the family being born twelve years after my brother. There had been another son who had died during the influenza epidemic of 1918 when he was only two years old. This little lad was never mentioned in the family. There were no photographs of him, and it was some fifteen years later that I was even told what his name was. He was called Joseph and the one and only story that I was ever told about him was a description of the family rushing out to an air-raid shelter during a Zeppelin raid in the midst of a bitterly cold winter's evening with the babe in my mother's arms. It could well be that the influenza which killed him was contracted that night but we shall never know.

I suppose that was one of the strange things about my family, their reluctance to tell me anything that happened before my birth. It was as though I was an unexpected visitor to the family - a visitor who had arrived late when all the arrangements had been organised and no information was necessary. The struggle to keep alive and to bring up three children to the point where they were ready to work and contribute to the family income was the task that preoccupied my parents, and they had almost completed that task, when along I arrived. Of course I received all the superficial trappings of filial attention, for that was in the Jewish tradition, and a point in my favour was that I was a boy, but I was never really drawn into the family bond. I always had to live inside, and yet outside, the family. It may be that my family were not really able to create this bond. They always seemed to me to be a collection of individuals sharing the same house. But how many other families operate like that?

My mother never spoke to me about her life before her marriage. Children are naturally curious about their parents. They want to perceive them as all-round human personalities, and they love to imagine their parents as children, hearing the tales of long ago. Later in life these stories may become boring but it fixes in the mind of the child that their parents had had an exciting or an eventful childhood. A mother's sense of humour, a father's impetuosity or bravery, a parent's fears, can be conveyed to the child reinforcing his or her own self-image, as well as enlarging the child's perception of how the family pattern came to be moulded and how one's own personality developed the way it did. But from my mother I got nothing.

I knew her maiden name — though how I discovered that I am not sure. Certainly she never told me. How she ever came to meet my father and why she ever married him I shall never know. Her command of the English language was almost non-existent and even after living in this country for over fifty years she was still unable to read one word. Her narrow world centred largely on herself and the constant struggle to survive on an insufficient income. Yiddish was spoken in the house though my brother and two sisters spoke to her in English. I can well remember the surprise and utter amazement when, at the age of about five or six, I went into a friend's house and heard his mother talking to him in English. Yes, an English-speaking Jewish woman. I had thought that only teachers spoke English!

To me my father was a more interesting person though I never really knew him very well. We were only drawn together for a very short period in 1939 before I joined the R.A.F. He had come from a town in the Ukraine, then called Ekatrinoslov, later named Zinovievgrad, and after the Stalinist purges, Kirovograd. His father was a rabbi who supplemented his income with a small distillery and two of the sons became rabbis. The family could not support any more children in full-time education, and so my father was sent out to learn one of the few trades open to Jews in prerevolutionary Russia. He became a cabinet maker but after only a few years he was conscripted into the Czarist army. Somewhere he met my mother, who was born in Kiev, and he decided to marry and leave the country to escape the awful humiliations he was receiving in the forces because he was a Jew. I believe he deserted, then travelled overland to Germany and then to England. His plan was to go to the U.S.A. but he settled in London for a while in order to work and save the fare to Liverpool and then to New York. He never got to Liverpool.

And this is about all that I know about my parents' early days, and all that I will ever know. How is it possible to grow up in a family and know so little about them? Why did they feel so shy and reserved, strangers, not only in this Country but to their own children. It must have been a traumatic experience for my mother, taken from her home in the Southern Ukraine, married to this soldier, who swept her right across Europe and then dumped her in a small room in the East End of London. My father had been born in 1878, my mother, I think, two years later, though no one knew for sure becuase no records were kept of births, it seems, in Russia amongst the Jewish poor. We certainly did not know any birthdays of my parents or their families.

My father and mother arrived in Bethnal Green in 1902. Bethnal Green, Whitechapel and Mile End, from the 1880s to the turn of the century, received tens of thousands of Jewish refugees, fleeing from the pogroms in eastern Europe, who arrived penniless and with a pitiful collection of possessions. Housing was cheap but atrocious but the Jews clung close together, opened little synagogues and helped one another to survive. Their experience of living in ghettos was put to good use here in England. The men brought their skills with them mainly in cabinet making, shoemaking and tailoring, and the more successful opened sweatshops to exploit the others. The women

Cyril's Mother and Father.

stayed in the house and never developed any skills or interests of their own. I never met any of my mother's acquaintances who did anything but domestic work. Their lives were very separate from that of their menfolk.

My father probably worked about fifteen hours a day. He was corresponding with one of his brothers who was living in New York and trying to make arrangements to go there. Over the years I did hear vague references to my father's family — I never knew their names or how many there were — but I understand that this particular brother had the means to assist my father to get to the U.S.A. But he never did and so our little branch of the family remained in England and my father settled down to make his life here. A daughter was born in 1904, another in 1907, and my brother in 1910.

Not very much of a family history. But I envied my schoolmates who could describe grandparents and even great grandparents and whose roots were firmly established in the contemporary cultural climate. I always felt inferior, very much the son of an immigrant. None of my friends could talk to my mother unless they understood Yiddish. In later years it became easier but in the early days of my childhood I was very much affected by this handicap.

Reaching back to those years reveals so little. I wish that I had great bucketfuls of memories, but I suppose mine was a dull little life for the first dozen years. The tin bath was my first memory. I can remember walking with my mother through a grey courtyard surrounded by grey flats (everything was grey in Bethnal Green) to school. I went to school in Rochelle Street at the age of three, probably because my mother wanted to be rid of me for a few hours each day. School was from nine till three thirty, and every afternoon little iron cots were set up in the hall and we had to rest on them. I hated this period of the day. I suppose that I was a pretty active child. My sister Rose always says that I was a handful and a menace.

Just about that time, my eldest sister Eva was married. She never really forgave my mother for having me, and was disgusted with the whole process of having this little child at her wedding. It took my father five years to recover from the expenses of the wedding and for the provision of the dowry. Eva moved away and

"Outside Rochelle school, Cyril: back-row, second from left".

I never saw a great deal of her after that. She never liked me, though in later years we did draw a little closer together.

My father's workshop, it could hardly be called a factory, was in Columbia Road, only a few hundred yards away from where we lived. Bethnal Green was a hotchpotch of slums, flats and houses juxtaposed with small workshops, so home life and working life poured into one another. It was easier for children, when they were old enough, to be absorbed into work and my brother, as soon as he was able, about the age of eleven or twelve, was drawn into the cabinet making industry, helping my father.

This little family unit was held together by its Jewishness. This pervaded the whole of my life, and was the most powerful single influence on me and my friends. Soon after my sister's wedding, we moved to a comfortable and spacious house in Meynell Road, overlooking Well Street Common, in Hackney. Although I never knew this we were living far beyond our means and when the crash came the family never recovered. It was the only period of affluence that I ever had. My father, now in partnership with an old friend, had his own factory, again in Columbia Road, employing some twenty or thirty people. It could, and should have been, a very successful business.

2   A Hard Day's Work

Most of the small furniture factories in the East End of London were run in the same way in the 1920s as they were when first established at the beginning of the century. As long as labour was cheap, and not very well organised, there was little impetus for change. The development of new technology only became apparent in the mid-thirties, and new materials and design not until after the 1939-45 War. For the mass market in furniture, as personified by the industry in East London, and no doubt repeated in other centres, in Manchester, Glasgow and elsewhere, production methods remained the same. The generation that came from Eastern Europe were a very conservative group, and worked in the same pattern as their own fathers had worked.

Workshops were badly lit, the floors uneven, heating was elemental, and hazards were great. I remember well one of the places where my father worked. The entrance was through a cobbled yard around which was a group of "factories", some producing clothes, some upholstery, and some, furniture. Men ducked through a narrow door into their workplace, the same door through which the finished furniture, often very bulky and bulbous, would be manoeuvred out, the same door through which timber would be delivered, or furnishing accessories and the dozens of other supplies would be delivered. It was unbearably hot in the summer, and incredibly cold in the winter. The thing that I remember most was the darkness and gloom of the place. How craftsmen ever operated in such appallingly lit conditions I shall never understand. The mistakes and shoddiness were all covered up and, although the furniture was made to last for years, there was much consumer dissatisfaction. I simply do not believe that "things aren't made as well now as they used to". At least, not with furniture!

Father's workshop was on three floors. Final assembly of the larger pieces, wardrobes, tallboys, dressing tables and the very large dining room tables and sideboards were assembled on the ground floor. There were large square holes cut out in each of the upper floors, with a primitive pulley system housed in the roof, through which timber was hauled up and the partly completed pieces of furniture were dropped down. There were no guards around these holes, just a cover, which was never put into place, leaving just a yawning gap in the middle of the production floor. The French polishers worked on the top floor — most of them were non-Jewish — and this was one of the lowest paid sections of the trade. A thin coating of veneer, usually oak, walnut, or maple, was applied to all flat surfaces and then polish was applied to give an opulent finish. It was this finish that sold the product, not the design. Gluepots would simmer over open fires all over the shop and the smell of this hot boiling glue and the different polishes that were being used was pretty horrific.

There was little contact between the French polishers and the rest of the work force. They stayed on the top floor to eat their lunch, which was heated up over the gluepots, tended to have their own Union organisation, and drank together in a different pub. Supervision was minimal, and there was no attempt to introduce any kind of quality control. Many a time my father or my brother Ben, had to commission a French polisher to touch up a piece of furniture in a shop or even in the home of a customer after it had been sold.

On the floor below, men were attaching ornamental legs, trimmings to chests, wardrobes, or cupboards, and other pre-carved attachments, which were brought in. Assembly and finishing took place on this and the ground floor. All the furniture was big and heavy and of one style, ornate, elaborate, and aping the beautiful work done by the craftsmen of the Eighteenth Century. Much of the timber came partially cut and planed from nearby sawmills which served dozens of such factories. Office administration and management went no further than paying wages and bills and getting orders.

My father was not very good at getting orders, or estimating prices, and Ben, when he joined this business at the age of 14, was even worse. There were two or three retailers in Whitechapel High Street, that would take completed bedroom or dining room suites at rock bottom prices and sell them at a considerable profit. Buying and selling was done on spec. Private orders were the best. These were largely obtained through personal recommen-dation, with a hefty commission changing hands, and my father would spend weeks haggling over the price to be charged, the delivery dates, and so on. Even after the order was completed it would be months before my father would be paid in full. As times got harder so father became more desperate to clinch a business deal and would even sell at a loss. The business, like so many others in the same position, was doomed to failure, and the ultimate destination of these small self-employed craftsmen, was into the large mass-production factories. My father's partner, Mr Haimovitch, was a much sharper and cunning business man who probably extracted far more from the business than his legitimate share. I would go into this strange world, from time to time, helping to push the wheelbarrows (when they were empty) from the timber yard to the workshop. The streets were full of these wheelbarrows being pushed from factory to factory. Horsedrawn vans were hired to take the completed furniture either to the retail shop or to the private house. Few could afford motor vehicles and, in any case, the location of the industry was a very tight one, confined to a few square miles.

So thousands of Jews eked out a precarious living, cheating one another, and united only in their attachment to their religion. A few began to apply modern production methods and move to more spacious premises in north London. Inspired by the second generation, better educated, and with a keener sense of business and commercial acumen, these young Jews left their parents behind in the East End, and moved on to the world of big business. Their doting parents would spread the stories of their success around, and increased the envy felt by those who were trapped in the endless treadmill of hard work and exploitation. I was only ten at the time, but could see it so clearly. I suppose my socialist spirit was born then. As the new large factories were established, the industry underwent a dramatic change. Trade unionism flourished, modern management in the form of budgeting and cost control was introduced, piecework replaced the old hourly rates and old craftsmen such as my father, exchanged their atrocious conditions and hours of work for an impersonal role in a large workforce, engaged in a production process that was largely assembling and finishing partly prepared production units of furniture.

3 Early Days At Home

Home in Meynell Road was a fairly quiet place. My father would leave the house very early, long before 7 a.m., and would be followed, rather reluctantly, by my brother an hour later after my mother and I had exhausted ourselves trying to get him to wake. This happened every morning. Neither they nor my sister Rose would return from work much before 8 p.m. We therefore ate practically all our meals separately. Week-ends were the only time the family sat down to meals together, and then even at these occasions, Rose was rarely present.

My father was an avid reader of newspapers. In those days he read Yiddish newspapers only. The one and only newspaper published in London was the Jewish Times, and he read it from cover to cover. We had to listen to him read the extracts, and never to criticize the content. My mother would be given it the next day, but I doubt if she read much of it. She rarely referred to anything in it, but spent long, silent hours pouring over it. After she had finished with it, the newspaper was handed on to a less fortunate friend who could not afford to buy a copy, and he, presumably, passed it on to someone else. The Jewish Times, under its editor Morris Myers, provided a unique service to the Jewish community, but when the number of Yiddish speaking Jews fell during the Thirties the paper collapsed. Although there were one or two feeble attempts by other publishers there never has been, nor ever will be, another Jewish Times. My regret was that we never saw the radical broadsheets produced in Yiddish. My father always kept away from the left-wing groups when he first came to England — although Lenin and Trotsky and others visited the Jewish emigre communities looking for support. So I guess that he must have been an Army deserter, though I can't be sure, and was afraid of being deported. The other great Yiddish paper was the American weekly, called "Forward". This had a picture supplement, with both Yiddish and English captions, which we seized on eagerly. As a small boy, I thought it rather glamorous to see this large paper, far bigger than newspapers printed in Fleet Street, shipped all the way from New York, with this supplement full of sepia coloured pictures.

Father used to collect this paper on Fridays. It had a large literary section that was often supplemented by the picture section. He would read us out long extracts from this section and we all had to listen. My mother would get bored with the "Lives of the Great Composers" or the condensed version of Thomas Mann's Buddenbrooks. My father really lived for his newspapers. I suppose that I have inherited that maniacal impulse to read every word of every newspaper and periodical that has come into my house, and my literary reading has suffered as a consequence.

But to return to my father. After our lunch on Saturdays, while my mother was washing up, he would regale us with readings. When I was very young, I marvelled at the knowledge my father had of the Classics — all gleaned from the pages of the "Forward". It was he who urged me to read Emil Zola, Dostoevsky, Thomas Hardy, Thomas Mann and others. He would read things twice and three times to us and if we protested that we had heard it before, he would shout and thump on the table. "Listen, you ignorant fools" he would say (in Yiddish, it would sound much worse) "and learn something." For my mother he would reserve his heaviest sarcasm. He would quiz her to find out which sections of "Forward" she had read. And the sparks would fly when he found out that she had missed something that he deemed important. As far as he was concerned, anything worth printing was worth reading. Old copies of the" Forward" went to the "shnorrers", scroungers, who called and asked for them regularly. There was never a shortage of these callers. Sadly, one day the "Forward" ceased to come into the house. I never did find out whether it had stopped publication, or whether my father could no longer afford to buy it. From then on, he read the News Chronicle, rather slowly at first, but very competently as time went on. The "Forward" was an old socialist paper, though it watered down its radicalism through the years. My father, however, never deviated from his support of the Labour Party until the day he died, much to the annoyance of many of his friends who had a fear of getting involved in British politics. He tried for years to try and educate my mother in all kinds of cultural and political interests, but gave up in the end. The 1945 General Election, that was the last straw. She stubbornly refused to go out and vote, and from then on he left her alone.

On Saturdays the workers would get paid at noon. Although my father was a boss he drew his wages at the same time as the others after which all the cabinet workers went off to the pub. He loved his beer, though he would only drink at weekends, which was all he could afford. It would be my job to try and bring him home for lunch. Invariably this meant my hanging around outside while he appeased me by buying me some sponge cakes. I thought these were simply out of this world, and I have very strong memories of standing outside on a patch of green grass, while he was inside busily treating everyone. I could not have been more than three or four at the time. He was incredibly generous and careless with money. When we finally returned, he rather merry, my mother rather angry, and the rest of us rather hungry, we would sit down to our Sabbath meal, which had been cooking since early morn, at about 3 p.m.

Although my parents were Orthodox Jews, they were not as strict as many of our neighbours. My father had to work on Saturday mornings for economic necessity, instead of going to the synagogue. He also worked on Sunday mornings. After dinner, he read us extracts from the Yiddish papers for an hour, then he would fall asleep, while my brother would lie down on his bed for a couple of hours. Saturday's routine was repeated on Sunday, except that the dinner was the remains of the previous day, heated up, and my brother slept for a longer period. God, how dull the weekends were! There was never a change in the routine, we never went anywhere and rarely had interesting visitors. The Jewish holidays were the exception. The atmosphere of the ghetto pervaded our lives. I was never allowed to see what another world was like. My friends were the sons of my father's friends. No one else was allowed in the house and so I learned the art of playing on my own. I invented hundreds of games and I treasured a box of dominoes which for many years was my only toy. My mother did not believe in toys, and my parents never bought me any. I did scrounge a few soldiers that boys in school discarded.

With such little social and cultural stimulation it is a wonder that I did anything at school in those early years. I taught myself to read at the age of four but it was to be another seven years before a book came into the house, and that was my one and only school prize. From 1930, the London County Council had stopped the issue of school prizes as an economy measure. So I made do with the Public Library. I went every week on Friday afternoons, no matter what the weather was like, for eleven years. If one includes two or three visits per week during school holidays, that makes about one thousand trips!

Cyril with his niece Lilyan.

I should mention my box of dominoes again. These became bricks to build houses, converted into battleships, and bi-planes, and farmland fences. But it must have been a fairly lonely childhood, my mother rarely spoke to me, and my sister and brother were far too superior to talk to their little brother. So I buried myself in my books and my dominoes. When I was five, my eldest sister had a daughter, and certainly my parents displayed far more interest and pleasure in their grandchild than ever they did in me. But to confound the psycho-analysts, I was never ever jealous and as my niece grew up I became very close to her. We have remained firm friends all our lives.

So this little Jewish boy grew up, having been told that he had been a nuisance when young, and became very quiet and circumspect. Life must have been so uneventful. I have so few memories of the days in Meynell Road overlooking Well Street Common. We lived there for five years, moving when I was eight, just as I had finished going to the Infants School. The house in Meynell Road was a large double fronted Victorian style house, and my bedroom, which I shared with my brother, was in an attic. On the top floor, where our tenants had a flat, there was a fairly rough wooden door. Behind that door was a steep flight of stairs that led to two attic rooms, the larger of which contained the cold water tank. This was the room that Ben and I shared, my sister slept in the other. We had a large double bed, and a huge wardrobe. I was terrified by this wardrobe and had horrible dreams which inevitably ended with this wardrobe descending on me. I suppose in the early days when I was three or four I was particularly scared and I remember many occasions when my sister had to sit with me. She was always very fed up and would try and leave as soon as she possibly could. I can never remember my mother ever coming up to comfort me or put me to bed. And, of course, men never bothered with children. Oh, how I used to hate going to bed! The noises in the tank as the water filled up upset me too. Why was mother so selfish? Surely a couple of minutes could have been spared for a rather lonely, frightened little boy, way up at the top of the house in the attic.

We never had a holiday. My mother flatly refused to sleep in anyone else's house and hotels were quite unknown. She would not eat in a house where the food might not be Kosher. She would not even travel so we never visited the countryside or the seaside. My father would go away occasionally on business, seeking

15

orders, and would stay with my brother-in-law's family in Birmingham or Glasgow, but my mother never travelled with him. I think that my first journey in a coach was when I was nine, and my first journey in a train was when I had reached the age of twelve. School holidays were pretty tedious, especially when those of my friends who could afford holidays went away. I can remember many hot and long summer days, when I played with a ball for hours on my own.

Moving from Bethnal Green in 1925 must have been a tremendous event for my family. I was too young to recognise it. They had lived there ever since coming to this country in 1901, and had been surrounded by their fellow Jewish immigrants. The old village "steitel" ties were strong and friendships were established when former neighbours and fellow townsfolk were reunited in London. There were a group of friends who were known as the Ekatrinoslavs. They had all come from the same town as my father. I didn't know their real surname for years, and they were the nearest to relatives that I had. The Ekatrinoslavs were a large family, four brothers and their wives, and a host of children, all much older than me. The eldest of the brothers, Abba, was a deeply religious man who never worked but pottered around the synagogue, the second was Shloma, a hard drinking, noisy, ebullient man, who was my father's best friend. My father and Shloma sank many a pint of Truman's ale, much to the disgust of my mother who disliked drink, noise and merriment of all kinds. The third brother, Shear, kept in the background and concentrated on his work. His three sons later built up their cabinet making into a very large manufacturing and retailing furniture business, and were eventually to employ my father when his own little business finally collapsed.

The fourth son, Adolphe, needs a paragraph or two to himself. In a world of fairly drab, hard-working and very conventional people, he presented a pretty romantic image, to me at any rate. Even his name captured my imagination. Adolphe was the youngest and was something of an intellectual. This made a ready appeal to my father who loved to talk about politics, philosophy and history with him. Adolphe was my godfather, although he hardly ever spoke to me and by the time I was ten he had disappeared. Adolphe was head and shoulders above his contemporaries. He could speak Russian and his English was quite good. He was the sales manager in the family business, and he and his wife had no children. In Jewish circles this was rare indeed. Consequently, he enjoyed a comfortable life and, through my child's eyes, he was fabulously rich. He was a Freemason and lived in a handsome house in Victoria Park Road in Hackney. On the rare occasions that I visited the house, I would be enthralled at the lush furniture, the bric-a-brac, and the best thing of all, the pianola. I thought this the last word in luxury. But not once was I given a sweet, or a biscuit or anything to eat or drink. Children were outside his world.

Adolphe and his wife went to lots of functions and, inevitably, Adolphe would be called upon to make a speech. These speeches were a subject of great discussion and comment throughout the whole community. Godfather he may have been to me — and this honour was bestowed on me, not him, and purely for snobbish reasons — but ignore me, he did. In fact, I cannot recollect what his wife, my godmother, looked like or what she was called. But there was a darker side to this flamboyant man. He was an alcoholic, though this was never mentioned, and he probably drunk himself to death. But none of this was allowed to sully his reputation or his memory.

Besides the close clannishness of the immigrants from the same towns was the hierarchy based on the country of origin. Everyone was a poor Jewish immigrant, working long hours for small wages, but where you were born was important. My parents were at the top of the pecking order. They came from Russia, though I believe the Muscovite Jews were grander than those from Odessa and the Ukraine. Below them, came the Poles. My mother would spit out the word "Pollack" when describing one she had encountered in a baker's queue. Below them were the Jews from the Baltic states of Latvia and Estonia, and then Roumania, at the bottom of them all. My mother had set her heart against any of her children marrying any Jew who was not Russian in origin. How far can prejudice go!

The question of marrying a non-Jew simply never occurred to her. We were just not allowed to have any non-Jewish friends. I never brought home any of my schoolfriends who were not Jewish, nor was I allowed to eat in their houses. Such was the degree of prejudice that existed, probably based on self-defence. The Jews were very vulnerable to anti-semetic outbreaks. After all, they had escaped from Eastern Europe because of that, and most of them had wanted to go to the U.S.A. where they felt that they really would be free. England was second best, and already the anti-Jewish feeling was growing as the post-war prosperity was receding.

4 The Jewishness of it all

So, in 1925, we were off. We moved to the large, spacious house in Meynell Road with a bathroom and a garden. My father's partner lived in the same road, and his family helped us to settle in. My father went off to the market in Columbia Road where his factory was and came back with boxes of plants. I can remember the unholy row that ensued when my mother went for him for wasting so much money on plants. She couldn't see the point of it. I know he was terribly enthusiastic and excited about this garden but I have a feeling that nothing was ever really cultivated. The garden was mostly a small square patch of grass, but he was oh so proud of his little plot of land and many a weekend afternoon he would lie on the grass and sleep his lunch off.

At the top of the house was the bathroom with a monstrous geyser which produced, amidst much noise, a tiny trickle of scalding water. We all bathed on Fridays, the only day that the geyser was lit and the tenants who occupied the first floor were not allowed to use it. That was not part of their agreement. We had a succession of tenants who all left owing my mother large amounts of rent. She was always too shy to ask them and my father could never be bothered to deal with such mundane domestic matters. He was never concerned with money. His partner, the wily bird, had five daughters, a calamitous position to be in because five daughters meant five lavish weddings, and five dowries, and he had to sweat and save hard. A further disadvantage was that none of his daughters were particularly attractive and already the eldest two were in their mid-twenties and as yet unmarried. Clearly the matchmakers had been unsuccessful.

We lived in this house in Hackney until 1930, when the onset of the Depression forced us to a much smaller house. The days of luxury — such as they were — were nearly over for my family but those years were fairly pleasant. We lived opposite the Common so I had green fields to play in instead of cobbled streets. On Saturday mornings I was allowed to go to Well Street Super Cinema with the three younger daughters of the partner up the road. The seats were two long hard benches in the front and admission was two pence. The noise and pandemonium were incredible, but we thought those comedies and the serials were great.

Every evening after school, and every Sunday morning, I would walk to the top of Well Street, about a mile away, to attend Hebrew classes. Going to Hebrew classes was mandatory, and there was no question of my being allowed to miss even one day. An older boy had been conscripted, most unwillingly, to go with me and bring me back, but he could never feel that it lay within his dignity to walk alongside this little boy. I had to run hard to keep up with him, and the return journey, often in the dark, was a particularly hazardous operation. These Hebrew classes were held on the top floor of a tenement block. The ground floor shops were in a derelict state, as were the flight of stairs that led to the rooms where the classes were held.

The Hebrew teacher, a wizened old man, would invariably arrive late, and we would all be sitting, all the way up the wooden stairs, waiting for him. Most of the boys were much older than me and I used to get more than my fair share of knocks, blows and kicks. My so-called protector never ever helped me. When the teacher finally arrived, smelling strongly of drink, he would usher us into the "schoolroom". This was a pretty bare room with some murky old desks and tables and an assortment of decrepit old chairs. The first ones in would grab the best of the chairs, the latecomers would have to squat on the floor. Attendance varied so there was no continuity in the instruction. The old teacher, who must have had a wretched life, would stand in front of us while we translated chunks of the Torah, and other prayers, whilst a general hubbub of noise went on all around. Since we were all fee paying students most of us adopted a fairly independent attitude to education which meant, in most cases, that the boys would play the old man up. After long bouts of ragging he would finally loose his patience and fling one or two boys down the stairs. I was very scared of his physical prowess, and witnessed several occasions when two or three boys would be thrown quite violently down two or three flights of stairs. After that a kind of uneasy peace would descend but then, mainly through sheer boredom, the noise would start again. The older boys who had to practise for their "Barmitzvah" would receive additional private lessons in their own homes. They needed it. So did he in order to supplement his meagre income. However, I managed to learn the rudiments of Hebrew and was able to read the prayers sufficiently well to satisfy my father when we went to the synagogue. I was safe for Judaism, and frequently at home during the Jewish festivals, would have to read the Prayer Book to my father. He would read it at the same time as me, correcting me constantly. I'd get very flustered, and his opinion of me as a devout Jew was shattered. It was never to recover.

Highlights were the Jewish festivals. Passover was grand because my mother would descend into the cellar and produce huge pots and pans and vast quantities of cutlery and crockery. None of this could be used at any other time of the year and all had to be thoroughly washed and scrubbed. The same intensive cleaning operation took place ten days later at the end of the Passover holiday. My mother worked herself into a frantic state to ensure that the whole house was cleaned from top to bottom. Curtains, rugs, cupboards were washed to perfection. The house had to be cleaned of any non-Kosher food. Not that we ever had any food or implement that carried the slightest suspicion of being other than Kosher but, for the Passover, all food that we ate had to bear the special label of the "Beth Din", the Jewish legal authority that supervised our dietary laws. Vast quantities of this special Kosher food were ordered, and for the next ten days, we were not allowed to eat any other kind of foods. Bread was forbidden and in its place were Matzos or unleavened bread.

My brother was always a good bread eater, and Matzos posed certain interesting problems for him. He was a sandwich eater par excellence and he would make fried egg matzo sandwiches, which had to be seen to be believed. Imagine a fried egg balanced very precariously between two flat sheets of matzo, which broke at the slightest pressure. Jam matzo sandwiches were easier to handle but used up a lot of jam, so a limit was imposed on these. The staple food we seemed to live on during this period was fried matzo. This was matzos dipped in eggs and poured into a frying pan and fried on both sides. My mother would stand over the cooker and fry these things for hours on end. The Passover frying pan was truly of gigantic proportions, I have never seen one before or since to match its circumference, and mother would pour in dozens of sheets of matzos dipped in eggs, and this would be fried until crispy. We had this for all meals from breakfast until supper. When freshly cooked, hot and sizzling, they were quite appetizing, being fried in chicken fat, but a slab of it cold and solid was quite daunting. It was guaranteed to lie on your chest for a week. I think my mother fried this stuff continuously for the whole ten days. Visitors would be offered a wedge in lieu of cake. Passover biscuits and cake were very expensive, and there- fore very special. They were reserved for distinguished visitors.

Cyril: "Barmitzvah Boy"

Certainly I wasn't allowed to have any nor did it ever occur to me to ask for one. We also had wine. It was the only time that we ever had drink in the house and again, it had to be the special Kosher Palestinian wine.

We also got new clothes for the festival. Although my birthday was three months before Passover, I used to get my birthday presents then. My birthday presents were always clothes, socks, shoes, trousers, a shirt. My father never knew my birthday; I don't think that my mother ever recorded a date on the calendar. She was only conversant with the Jewish days and months of the year, and my brother and sister rarely recorded my birthday. So my presents came on Passover; clothes bought in the little East End shops owned by friends and acquaintances. Everything was bought in this way, mostly on credit, and as a result of strong bargaining. Often the shopkeepers would call on us in our home with their goods, touting for sales. My feet are forever deformed as a result of the boots and shoes that I was forced to wear, bought very cheaply from some bootmaker acquaintance, as a present! Besides the wine and the food, another innovation were nuts. We had little Spanish nuts, which also served the purpose of an important game. These nuts would be rolled up the pavement. If we hit the marker, then all the nuts on the ground would be won. This was the forerunner of the games of "Flicking" with cigarette cards. In this game, also played in the streets, or school playground, three cards would be propped up against the wall whilst the players flicked another card with forefinger and thumb to try and knock down the three cards. The boy who knocked down all three would collect all the cigarette cards that lay on the ground.

The years were marked by these festivals, which brought the only dash of colour to our lives. Otherwise the weeks were much the same and Xmas and Easter were quite unknown to me. It is hard to visualise what a closed world we lived in, and how fiercely my mother guarded this world.

The Jewish New Year and Yom Kippur meant long days in the synagogue. There were a number of palatial and ornate synagogues in Hackney, supported by the wealthy by an annual subscription. Giving additional donations entitled them to a seat during the High Festival as it was called. The greater their donation the more prestigious a seat they would get. We, of course, were in no position to make any kind of donation of the order required. We went to one of the temporary synagogues set up in adjoining halls. The one we went to in Shore Road had a makeshift altar, rather like a broom cupboard, and then row upon row of chairs lined up opposite it. Very different from the ornate and religious majesty of the synagogue next door in Devonshire Road. My father took his responsibilities very seriously and became a devout Jew for the duration of these Festivals. We would leave the house at 8 a.m. and walk to the synagogue, carrying our prayer books and prayer shawls in a little velvet bag. Luckily I was with my father and so avoided the taunts of the non-Jewish boys who, of course, were going to school.

The synagogue was hot, stuffy and noisy. The cantor seemed to be singing and praying to himself. I was not allowed to leave the service even to go to the lavatory. As the morning wore on, so the tedium increased. Most of the men would discuss business and relate stories about their acquaintances. This was an annual gathering and reunion for many who only met each year, for the congregation rarely varied and everyone kept to the same seats. Every so often the beadle would clap his prayer book and call for silence when the noise got too loud, but it would not be long before the chatter would start again. My father would really enjoy these discussions, and his loud laughter would make me colour up. I always kept one eye on the beadle. There was one serious point in the service when members had to give up special prayers for the dead. I, and most of the youngsters who had no dead parents, would have to leave the service and wait outside. For many, this was an excuse to flaunt their new clothes, or to chat up the young girls attending the main synagogue. In our religion women were completely segregated, and — except for brief periods — rarely attended the services. In any case they were busy at home preparing the table.

I can remember the pangs of hunger and the agony of that last hour of the service. Often we would be invited into a friend's house for a glass of wine and a piece of sponge cake which would delay our homeward trek for at least another hour. Lunch was taken about 3.30 invariably accompanied by my mother's grumbles about the dinner being spoilt. The Day of Atonement, however, was different for on this day my mother spent the day in the synagogue. From the age of twelve I was obliged to fast for the whole day as well as spending all the time in the synagogue. Yom Kippur would start the night before with a hefty meal before we went off to the synagogue but in the morning my mouth would be dry and yet I could not as much as brush my teeth. My mother would make heavy weather of the fast and wilt visibly. I was always afraid that she would faint. Slowly the day wore on until about 6 p.m. when the fast was over, and we could leave the synagogue. My brother would pull an apple out of his pocket and munch it on the way home. Although this happened every year, I was still flabbergasted at the sudden appearance of this food. As a little boy, I was convinced that the Heavens would open if any adult was found carrying food of any description on Yom Kippur.

Religion had an all embracing influence on me, in fact, terrorized me. I was a very impressionable lad. My brother-in-law Sam, had a complete set of the Children's Encyclopedia which I was allowed to look at only under supervision and only at special times. In every volume there was a section on the world's art treasures and, of course, there were reproductions of the early masters depicting the Crucifixion, the Birth of Jesus, the Virgin Mary, etc. I could not, and would not, look at these pictures. If I did terrible harm would be wreaked on me! And so I followed the traditional, orthodox pattern of behaviour, unthinkingly and unquestioningly. My mother made sure of that. The only occasion when we were really let loose and when there was a fun element in all this business, was during the Feast of Tabernacles which followed a couple of weeks after Yom Kippur. This was a jolly festival, when all the children were given sweets after the service. The grander the synagogue, the better the sweets. The top synagogue in Hackney distributed boxes of chocolates and, if you were quick enough, and smart enough, you could go round twice. One or two boys would boast of having collected three boxes. Of course, if you were recognised as coming up for a second time you would get a hefty cuff on the ears and a threat to see your parents. The other trick was to collect one packet and then race off to another synagogue and, providing that they had not finished their distribution, innocently line up and get another one. It was important for me to get as much as I could for I rarely ever got any money to buy sweets, especially in those early days. My brother occasionally brought me an ice-cream during the long hot summers that seemed an integral part of my early childhood. What does the passage of time do to Man, that makes him dream that the summers of his childhood and his youth were always hot and long and glorious? For me that is so. The summers of the Thirties were grand as was that ice-cream. They came in thick, creamy slices, were sold from a barrow and were made by Joe Assenheim.

The man selling the ice-cream would call out "Assenheim, Assenheim" as he pushed his barrow down the road. Half a slice cost a halfpenny, and was wrapped in white paper. Even these half slices were too big for me and I would have a small chunk of this superb creamy concoction. The barrow man would sell his ice-cream at all hours — far into the night.

The sweet shops and the newsagents hardly ever closed. I would be sent off, firstly in Brick Lane then later in Well Street, at all hours to bring cornets for my brother and sister and, although I was never allowed any myself, I would make sure that I had enough lickings on the way back. They never suspected that I had already sampled the goods. I used to enjoy going into these shops. There was always a crowd of people in there gossiping and, although it was always in Yiddish, I could understand everything. Besides, there was always the chance that someone who knew me would treat me to a chewy sweet. I only told my mother once about these gifts and she berated me about accepting gifts, only "shnorrers" did that. Like many people of limited means she carried her poverty with pride, sensing some sort of virtue in poverty. I was always ready to run errands, a job I was to do frequently throughout my childhood, though in later years it did become more irksome. It was no fun as a teenager, to go off to the Library in Mare Street to choose books for an elder brother, or to rush off to the chemist shop to get razor blades for him, and so on.

About my early schooling, alas, I can remember very little. I was taken out of my first school as it was "too rough", a euphemism for describing an anti-semitic atmosphere, and I was sent to another school which had a higher proportion of Jewish children where we could rely on the protection of the older boys. But these early years at school passed me by. Certainly I do not retain memories of a happy or a lively experience. However, I was getting a reputation for being bright though destructive.

My brother had bought a new radio, or wireless as it was called then, in 1928. It had a clock incorporated in it, and it was a big black portable box, which sat on the corner of the kitchen table, the pride and joy of my brother and sister. One day, I succumbed to temptation and opened the box. I touched the clock to find out how it worked. The clock stopped and never worked again. I certainly was in trouble and it was years before I ever touched the controls of a radio again. That was when my mother, who never ever learned to operate a radio or a television set, wanted to listen to Henry Hall.

We moved to Clapton in 1930, to Newick Road. My 53 tram route theory was beginning to work out. This tram route, later superseded by the 653 trolleybus, ran from Aldgate, through Hackney, Clapton and Stamford Hill, to Tottenham Court Road — a route from the East End to the West End of London. As people became more successful or affluent they would leave the East End and make for the newer, rather grander houses in Stamford Hill. Their parents would remain behind in the East End but the 53 route was the link. Private cars were few and far between, and so public transport was paramount. The 53 tram, and the 653 trolleybus, had just as important a colonisation effect on the Jews of London as did the Bakerloo Line for suburbia. Later, of course, the Jews who amassed greater wealth or prestige would move off to the North West London suburbs. But to me, moving to Clapton was a step forward. My father's business seemed to be flourishing but this was 1930, and the Depression was soon to hit us.

"Cyril with Mother and Father"

5   A Yiddishe Momma

I can never understand how and why my mother married my father. She was a typical Yiddishe Momma. As far as I was concerned, she was always a little, old, rather fat, grey-haired lady who rarely smiled and was continually complaining about the pains in her feet and legs. She suffered rather badly from corns, and would purchase a lotion called Union Jack to rub in on her swollen feet and legs with great regularity. I don't think it really helped, but she persevered all through the years, suffering, but making sure we all knew about it. I used to pray to God every night to make her legs better but God never replied. I was scared that she would die and leave me motherless but she lived for another forty years and died in her mid-eighties.

She was a shy person who put up with a great deal of banter from my father. As with all women who come from a backward, semi-literate society she buried herself in unending domestic chores. She was passionately houseproud and spent hours scouring and polishing our ancient gas cooker. As a cook, I found her wanting. Like all her contemporaries she basked in the self-congratulatory atmosphere of producing good wholesome home cooking for, after all, that was what being a mother was all about. My mother's knowledge of recipes was pretty limited. Somehow she had achieved a reputation of being a good cook. Certainly my sisters and brother affirmed this and, in her defence, would say that in days gone by she had produced magnificent meals. I would be constantly reminded of the fact that I had arrived late, almost too late, on the family scene. Everything that was worth happening to the family had already happened. Although I had not appreciated that I was unplanned I soon realised that I was in the way. Everyone around me was so old, my parents, their friends, and the sons and daughters of their friends.

My mother's limited range of recipes meant that each day of the week for us meant the same meals. She cooked the Sabbath meal on Saturdays, a non-meat meal on Mondays, a meat dish on Tuesdays and fish on Thursdays. In between those days we had the previous meal heated up. How we survived, in the days before refrigerators, without being food poisoned is a mystery to me. Fish cakes, cooked on Thursday, would be kept in the pantry and eaten on Sunday and even on Monday. We rarely had puddings and, since the dietary laws forbade the mixing of meat and milk, never had custard or cream. Only on the non-meat days did we have milk puddings and jelly and custard was a rare treat which appeared on some Thursdays after fish. Year in and year out we ate our way through the same dishes, the same vegetables and the same tired old recipes.

The Jewish Chronicle, a weekly which was too expensive for us to buy and which I occasionally saw in a friend's house, carried a cookery column, edited for countless years by Florence Greenberg. Years later, when I was a student at the L.S.E., I met Naomi Greenberg, her daughter who was a fellow student, who invited me home to the family flat for tea. I looked forward with quiet anticipation to the joys of good Jewish cooking. We got a cup of tea and a slice of Lyons Swiss Roll! My mother, of course, never read any recipes nor discussed cooking with her friends. She was a grumbler who complained ceaselessly about the monumental stack of domestic chores that engulfed her.

Most of the time it was just the two of us at home. My father, Ben and Rose all worked a ten-hour day, and so it was quite late before they returned home in the evening. And yet my mother never sat down to talk to me, or confide in me in any way. I grew up side by side with her, both of us as strangers to one another. It seems incredible to me now but she was such a negative character. Rarely did any emotion pass over her face. For me she remained the archetypical long-suffering female housebound worker. She was fiercely obstinate, and carried all the superstitions and prejudices of her Russian peasant origin right through until the day she died. Sex was never mentioned, Christians (Goyim) were taboo, men had to be waited on, humour was undignified, routine was all important, controversy was to be avoided and one's poverty had always to be hidden. Yet she was not a hard woman. Love and affection she found hard to show, and yet she was caught up in the terrible game, beloved by all these Jewish Mommas, of extolling the virtues of their sons and daughters to friends and neighbours. My mother had very little to boast about. We were all very ordinary. The biggest crime was to marry out of the Jewish faith, and so all my friends were vetted to ensure not only that they were Jewish but that they had Kosher homes. By the time that I was growing up adherence to the Jewish dietary laws was relaxing a little but my mother was not going to let her standards fall. We walked together a lot. To my married sister

Eva's house in Belgrave Road, to the market, to friends. She walked very slowly, and with some difficulty, and from a very early age I learned to hold her arm and to help her along. To me she was always suffering and, under her influence, I became rather a solemn and introspective young boy. There was no opportunity for jumping, hopping and skipping along the road. Yet I was never unhappy. The strong wall of Judaism protected me. I was a member of the Chosen People and could feel superior to all those people around me in spite of the cries of Volla, Volla Jewboy that taunted me. This was the favourite cry of the schoolboys around, many of whom may only have vaguely been aware of anti-semitism, but it was an oft-repeated cry nevertheless. My mother's cooking, her embargo on my playing any games and indeed following any active pursuit or hobby, meant that I became a rather plump young boy. I remained grossly overweight until I left school, and only my years in the R.A.F. brought my weight down to something approaching normal. I remember being eight stone when I was eight and eleven stone when I was only a little older than eleven.

The only time that she ever stopped working was late at night when she would put on her reading glasses, purchased from Woolworths and replaced every five or six years, and laboriously read pieces from the "Jewish Times". Of course as the years went by and her familiarity with written Yiddish declined, she found it more difficult to read for any length of time. Television came too late for her to develop an interest or enthusiasm, and so her relaxation would be to sit and reflect. Reflect on what, I wonder? It was as if she was waiting for death almost as soon as she was born.

My mother was a prisoner of her times and lacked the strength, time, intelligence and spirit to break out. As a result she withdrew into her own protective shell and feared the outside world. An immensely shy person, she could never communicate. So sadly these pages show a non relationship between myself and her. But I did not intend this to be a sexist portrait. I have described my mother as I remembered her, how she appeared to me and to others. A majority of immigrant Jewish women shared completely the life experience of their families and made major contributions to the development and progress of their family. True, my mother provided me with a stable, albeit colourless home and worked eighteen hours a day to ensure that we were fed, clothed and washed and that the creditors were kept at bay. It is true that she had uprooted herself from her childhood home, her friends and family and set up in a foreign country with its completely alien culture. That showed great strength. But that was all. The move to England seemed to have drained all her personal initiative and individuality and she was unable to come to terms with her life in England.

6 A Night Out in the Theatre

A great experience was going to the theatre. My father loved the theatre and my greatest gift to him was when, after I had just been demobilised, I took him to see Peter Ustinov give a stunning performance as Raskolnikov in "Crime and Punishment". It was his first and only visit to the English theatre. The Jewish Pavilion in Whitechapel Road was the major Yiddish theatre in the U.K., though there were one or two other smaller and seedier ones that were barely surviving in the '20s. The Yiddish theatre in the U.S.A. was extremely strong and in fact such movie stars as Pall Muni had started on the Yiddish stage. Very occasionally an American actor or director would visit England, and my father would always endeavour to get seats for these performances. He was for ever reminiscing about the great performances of the past, of Morris Shwartz's "Tevye the Milchiger" (Fiddler on the Roof), of Morris Moscowitch's "Shylock", and other masterpieces. However, the Jewish Pavilion was more like a circus than a theatre.

Firstly, there was the noise. Everyone talked incessantly, just the same as in the synagogue. Friends would meet and, irrespective of the numbered seats, would sit together. This would evoke immediate protests and arguments when the legitimate seat holders arrived and claimed their rights. These arguments were going on all over the auditorium. There was a large snack bar, unlicensed, where piles of rolls, sandwiches and bagels filled with smoked salmon or cream cheese, were sold. Everybody was eating. We couldn't afford these goodies, but my mother would bring a huge picnic with her, and the three of us would eat solidly throughout the performance as was everybody else. The noise was devastating. People eating, muttering approval or disapproval of what was going on on the stage, and explaining to those who could not understand what was going on, or to those who were unable to follow the intricacies of the plot. My father was especially guilty of this. He loved to give his interpretation of what was happening, to people in the row in front and behind as well as those sitting by his side. This he would do in a very loud whisper whilst my mother would shush him as did most of the audience around.

Everyone on stage overacted like mad. The audience loved it, and the more dramatic and hammy the performance, the more rapturous the applause that followed. Most of the plays seemed to revolve around the tearful mother pleading with her daughter not to leave home. Comedies and modern plays were few and far between. The audience liked to be reminded of life in eastern Europe before the first World War, and nostalgia and sadness had to be the dominant themes. During the intervals, which were very long and very frequent, people would promenade, eat, talk and survey one another's clothes. Again there was one-upmanship in the seat you had. People would change seats willy-nilly, provoking more arguments and noise, whilst others would appeal for calm and order, as the curtain had risen and the next act was under way. My father was a terror. He would simply forget the seat that he had had and would return to the nearest one he fancied. It was no use either my mother or I telling him he was in somebody else's seat. He just would not budge. It was his seat.

At the end of the play, there would be a very long speech full of theatrical flourishes and quite a performance in its own right, when the principal actor gave a fairly comprehensive account of the next play that would be performed and urged the audience to come and support it. Support it they did until the German bombers destroyed the Pavilion in the Blitz. There is no Yiddish theatre in Britain today, no more Victorian melodramas, no quarrelling over the rightful possession of seats, and above all no noise in the auditorium. My father, on his visit to the West End theatre, was visibly impressed. It was so quiet and so orderly.

Entertaining or visiting friends was the only other social event of my childhood. There were no babysitters, and my brother and sister were not interested in sitting in, so I went everywhere with my parents. I always walked with my mother, helping her along, whilst my father would walk on ahead. He couldn't bear to keep down to my mother's slow pace. Consequently they rarely spoke to one another, and I had no chance of talking to my father. Communication wasn't the strongest feature of our family. We all seemed to live our own lives, sheltering behind our own thoughts.

My mother had a set pattern for entertaining which father thought magnificent. She would boil dozens of potatoes in their jackets and serve pickled and cured brown herrings and moun-tains of rye bread and cream cheese. That was the supper, served in the same way for 40 years. As long as the potatoes were cooked things were fine, but how my father would shout if they were hard. The potatoes would be peeled and eaten piping hot with herrings and bread. Then the men would play cards which invariably led to violent arguments and recriminations. Friendships were shattered as a result of these card games but still they went on. It was incredibly boring for me but at least I could crawl off to bed at a reasonable time. The only consolation when we went to my parents' friends' houses was the more lavish hospitality and that I could sample someone else's much better cooking. I really hated the potato and herring suppers. And yet no one else in the family ever did any cooking. Neither of my two sisters even had the faintest interest or ability in cooking and, when I was married, I carried only knowledge of making custard, porridge, boiling an egg and making tea. My father never even cut a slice of bread during the whole of his life. My mother reigned absolutely supreme in the kitchen. Nor was there ever any attempt to lay the table. Knives and forks were just pushed on to the table, along with the plates, and hot lemon or Russian tea.

Millfield Road school: Cyril is second row from front, near right

7 Early Years in Clapton

We now lived in Clapton, which at the end of the '30s still displayed an air of gentility. The streets were clean and we boasted a Tory M.P., Sir Austin Hudson. My father, who had become naturalised, almost the first of his circle of friends to do so, regarded his citizenship with pride and voted in every election, never wavering in his support for Labour.

Life changed for me. The world opened up a little. I joined yet another school, my fourth, Millfield Road School, and my opening remark to boys I liked was "Are you Jewish?". I really was conditioned. Only if the answer was in the affirmative was the relationship to be continued. Otherwise the boy was to be avoided. I had new friends who were allowed to enter my house, we had Jewish neighbours, with whom I could converse and I had one woman teacher who I thought was absolutely marvellous. The system in this primary school was that the teacher moved up with the class, so Mr Bristow became very familiar with all of us. Although it was a mixed juniors the boys and girls had separate playgrounds and the sexes were kept fairly well apart in class. Most of the learning was by rote. Mr Bristow would put large charts over the blackboard and we would all sing out in unison the Kings and Queens of England, the Rivers and Towns of Britain, the multiplication tables and so on. We sat at the same desks in the same classroom all the time we were there. There was little or no movement anywhere and we marched in lines to and from assembly, to the cloakrooms and to the playground.

It was impossible to behave as an individual. The only time we were allowed to relax was the last day of term when we could bring our own books and toys in. I found this rather difficult as I had so little of my own and Bristow used to vent his sarcasm on me. Although I was the brightest child in the class I was fat, Jewish and bad at games so he didn't think a lot of me. However, I enjoyed my early schooldays; there were lots of books to read which supplemented by library reading.

I used to go to the barber's shop every fifth or sixth Friday to have my hair cut. Barber shops were a world of their own. The men, chattering all the time whilst wielding scissors and razors, seemed highly sophisticated. Many of the customers stayed there for hours talking to one another mainly about sport in general and horse and dog racing in particular. Boys were scorned. They were a nuisance and they didn't give tips. So our hair was cut as quickly as possible. As we were rather small to sit in the large barber's chairs, a plank would be placed over the arms and we would be sat on that. As soon as a youngster reached a certain height he would have to stand on the floor at the back of the chair.

One afternoon I was beckoned over by one of the barbers, told to stand behind the chair and a white sheet was flung over my shoulders. He told me to stand straight, not to move, and to put my hands behind my back. This was the usual instruction. I soon realised that he had taken his penis out and was pressing it against my hands. I was absolutely terrified, not allowed to move whilst he stood there close up against me and cut my hair. This torture went on for twenty minutes. I paid and rushed out, still feeling his damp penis on my hands. I told no one about this, not that I knew what it was all about, but I couldn't bring myself to go to that barber's for weeks. I was terribly scared and, in the end, when my mother forced me to go, I saw that barber there. To my intense relief he didn't cut my hair, but I suffered agonies in case this should happen again. Sex did not rear its ugly head again, not in our house anyway!

Right until 1939, when my brother got married, we shared the same bedroom and, in fact, the same bed; a large double bed that had been made by my father soon after the first World War. Eventually when we lost our bedroom we used a "Put-U-Up" in the front room which put paid to any pretensions about having a dining room since this became a bedroom with clothes deposited over the chairs and the table. And yet all those years of close proximity did not draw us together. I, of course, admired my big brother from afar, ran all his errands for him, and yet when I was to meet him in 1981 after a period of ten years, he confessed that he never knew me. That shook me since I held him in such high regard and assumed he had some feelings for me. I shouldn't have been shocked for of course it was true.

We all took the 11-plus examination and, although I was pretty confident I would pass, we were still on tenterhooks waiting for the results. Old Bristow basked in the power he had to withhold the information for half a day. Eventually he condescended to read out the list of successful pupils and then told the lucky few they could go home early to tell their mothers the important news. I flew home as fast as I could and breathlessly knocked on the door. No one was in and, in a state of anti-climax, I sat on the doorstep for an hour until my mother returned from the shops. She promptly admonished me for sitting outside like some orphan and, suitably deflated, I came in and told her the news. The others who were successful received presents for passing the examination — watches, bikes, fountain pens. I received nothing and was plunged into a long family discussion on whether or not I should go to the grammar school. None of my parents' friends had children who had been to a grammar school; it was the cost of the school uniform and the consent for me to stay at school until I was sixteen that were the stumbling blocks. Eventually my married sister said emphatically I should go: there would be a small grant called The Junior County Scholarship that would help and she would also give me sixpence a week pocket money when I started in September. So off I went to the Grocers Company School — Hackney Downs Grammar School — with a £9 a year Scholarship grant paid into a brand new Post Office Savings Book and sixpence a week from my sister which lasted for all of twelve years.

8 The Years of Depression

Two months after this and before I made my way to the grammar school we had moved again. One of the reasons for the lengthy debate on whether I should take up the Junior County Scholarship award was the fact that my father's business had crumbled. The recession had gripped Britain and the furniture industry fared no better than any other industry. My father had been forced some two years previously to break up his partnership and from the remains of the wreckage, salvaged enough tools and equipment for him and my brother to continue on their own. Their little workshop was a deathtrap by the canal in Islington. They relied almost entirely on private orders but who on earth would call there to place an order. Customers were mostly friends of the family whose daughters were getting married and who wanted a bargain. After two years of this hand to mouth existence, and my father was not alone in remaining in this precarious state, he finally went bankrupt and both he and my brother went to work for someone else, the Ekatorinoslavs.

It must have been a tremendous blow to my father's pride, after thirty years as a Master Cabinet Maker, to be an employee. He was now in his mid-fifties but the Ekatorinoslavs treated him kindly and employed him. I don't suppose he was the easiest of employees. He certainly didn't take orders kindly but these were sad years for him. He didn't even have the dignity of being a foreman. My brother was worked twice as hard as he had ever been in one of the modern furniture factories in Enfield producing mass-produced furniture rather cheaply and shoddily. Craftsmanship went out of the window and my brother, if he had ever been any good, soon lost his artistic skills.

There had always been beggars on the streets of London. Many were disabled ex-servicemen who displayed their medals in a pathetic and self-conscious way. I can remember one such person who terrified me, and I did all I could to avoid him. He of course hardly saw me for he was almost totally blind, was dressed in rags, had a withered arm, and sang in an evil, croaking voice. He always stood in the same spot on Lower Clapton Road, at the corner of the road where we then lived, and arrived at daylight and stayed until it was dark. He never moved but croaked out some meaningless song. He stood at that pitch long after we had moved from the area, this Dickensian figure, a reminder of the squalor and poverty that was around. Although we were never far from poverty at home and at school, there was around us plenty of evidence of the tens of thousands who were much more unfortunate than us.

Our standard of living went down sharply; gone was the bathroom and the house we now rented in Kenninghall Road had only one outside lavatory. Even so we shared this little three-bedroomed house with another family who had two girls. We no longer went to Jewish weddings and other festivities, which had provided a feast of memories for me as a child, because we could no longer afford the clothes or the presents. How can one begin to describe these weddings, being conducted all over London and the major cities of Britain where Jews lived? Movement was restricted and most marriages were between people who lived in the same area, and almost certainly from the same town. Many of the marriages were the work of marriage brokers who would arrange meetings through the parents. Certainly by the time a daughter had reached her mid-twenties and was still unmarried there would be long anguished meetings of anxious parents with these brokers. The final settlement included not only the dowry, but the type of wedding that would be provided. A wedding was a financial transaction. The bride's father invested heavily in order to recoup status and reputation for himself and get appropriate wedding gifts for his daughter. The grander the wedding, the more impressive the gifts had to be. We had to drop out of this circuit in 1932 and refused most invitations. My sister's wedding, the result of a matchmaker, put paid to this. So many contemporaries of my father were in the same boat — they refused invitations to attend my sister's rather modest wedding party and so we reciprocated.

But the weddings, before that — they were vivid in my memory. About a dozen Kosher caterers would prepare these functions — each in a descending order of luxury and expense. Long before you received the invitation (itself an indication of the price tag), you knew who was going to do the catering, and how expensive this was going to be.

Hired cars would collect the guests and take them to the bride or bridegroom's house for early morning drinks. The tables would be groaning with food, sweets, chocolates, cakes and drinks. In the post mortem that followed my mother and her friends would recall every scrap of food that had been offered. My father would get merry quite quickly on whisky and would grab handfuls of chocolates which he distributed to the children standing outside the house, and watching great limousines extruding expensively dressed men and women into the tiny house, transformed for this festive occasion. The cars would take the guests to the synagogue for the service and thence on to the wedding breakfast. The reception — taken about 3 p.m. — would be preceded by drinks and cakes and chocolates and savouries. I was usually quite full by the time we came to this four or five course meal, nearly always the same as many of the previous functions. One thing was certain, you knew exactly what you were going to eat. Only the number of courses changed, in accordance with the amount paid. The guests then retired home to change into evening wear and returned for dinner, dancing and supper. And throughout the day the drinks flowed, everyone over-ate and apologised for abandoning their diet and gossiped. But for me it brought a touch of glamour. I must have gone to about fifty or sixty of these weddings during the '20s and a further seven or eight during the '30s, and none, thank goodness, after that.

The purpose of these weddings was not only to impress and to create some kind of financial return for the married couple, but also to fasten them more closely to the world of Jewry. There were no weddings for those who chose to marry Christians, even if they took up the Jewish faith, not in orthodox Jewish circles. So it was also an affirmation of Jewishness, an assertion to the hostile world outside that Judaism still flourished. My brother broke with convention by getting married and holding the reception in a small West End hotel, and not in the conventional Jewish caterer's hall. But then this was in 1939, and things were changing...

But we must return to 1933, the year I went off to grammar school, the year my father went off to the Bankruptcy Court, the year we returned to taking our weekly bath at the Hackney Public Baths. We would walk there on Friday afternoons, pay twopence for a second class ticket and if you forgot your towel, one further penny for a rather threadbare towel with Hackney Borough Council emblazoned all over it. The bath attendant was one of those terrifying ogres who, like all park keepers, synagogue beadles and school caretakers, hated children. We sat in a tiny uncomfortable room on wooden benches and waited for our turn. Fridays and Saturdays were always busy days and the waiting period was very lengthy, often two or three hours.

The baths themselves were large with wooden surrounds. The bath attendant, dressed in shabby white trousers and a decrepit white short jacket and wellington boots, would march up and down the aisle between the rows of cubicles swinging his water key. He would show you into a bath cubicle, awash with water which he sluiced around as a substitute for cleaning out after the previous occupier. With a twirl of his key, scalding hot water gushed out, and you locked the door and undressed. A few seconds later, the water stopped. In vain you called out "more hot, number 10". No one took any notice of kids, certainly not in the second class. So you attempted to wash in a couple of inches of scalding water. Occasionally your cries would be answered and a further stream of water would arrive, either very very cold or very very hot. A few minutes later there would be a fierce banging on the door, a shout "out number 10" and the plug would be opened and you lost the water. And then came the long walk home.

I wasn't a very bright scholar at grammar school. In fact had my family realised how moderately I was performing I would have been taken out long before I was sixteen. The school tried to impose middle-class standards on Jewish working-class culture and did not succeed. Since I wasn't any good at games and my parents just did not believe in the need to buy any form of sports equipment, that part of school life was denied me and I was always on the outside watching people play games. In any case the school playing fields were three or four miles away in Edmonton and the boys used to travel there by train to practice and play. I only went three times, to the Annual Sports Day, only three trips by train, one of which, when I was twelve, was that first journey ever on a train!

9 Life at Grammar School

We had a two mile walk to school and a couple of my friends called for me every day and we picked up a few more on the way across the Hackney Downs. School uniform presented a problem for my parents. The grant I received was supposed to cover it, but I made do with the school cap and a badge, which was sewn on to my jacket in lieu of a blazer, and a tie. We were a boisterous noisy lot going to school and one of our group, nicknamed Sally, suffered greatly. Many times his cap was flung into the ladies lavatory, and he, with tears of humiliation in his eyes, would have to descend into the mysterious toilets to recover it. Poor old Sally, he had a dreadful time at school but he is now a very eminent professor of Sociology at one of our major Universities.

My mother refused to allow me to eat at school. Even sandwiches were not allowed, as she feared the food might be contaminated by the school's non-Kosher plates, so I trekked back at lunchtime every day, often on my own. Four times a day, five days a week, through all weathers. For over five years I did that journey to a school I began to dislike more and more as time went on.

Sarcasm was the main weapon used by the less tolerant staff and we retaliated by ragging the weaker members who, in the end, were forced to resort to corporal punishment or very stiff sentences of detention. Since the Jewish boys were not allowed to come in on Saturdays for detention, they would have to stay on after hours during the week, a move which was not highly regarded by the staff who had to put in a couple of hours of unpaid overtime.

The school played soccer — it was not prestigious enough to play rugger — but we had a cadet force and everybody did rifle drill with heavy wooden dummy rifles. We marched, paraded and drilled weekly and, every few months, the whole school marched behind the band and the colours, along the Hackney Downs, with the Headmaster taking the salute. It was there that quite a number of members of the British Union of Fascists learned their military discipline. We had quite a few fascists in the school who readily provoked the Jewish boys, and as Mosley's paramilitary forces grew, so they joined as leading lieutenants. I suppose some of the staff were fairly sympathetic to the fascists. They were fed up with the arrogance and self-confidence displayed by some of the brighter, more intelligent young Jews. There was never any political discussion, never a debate on the rise of Hitler's Germany and its implications for European peace. We had to leave that outside the hallowed walls of the school.

Jewish parents were realising the social advantages of grammar school education, and were pushing their children to higher attainments. Their sons were being directed towards the professions, mainly law and medicine. These were high status and hopefully the most rewarding financially. Long before Prof. Halsey discovered the contribution that education made in terms of social mobility, these artisan Jews had already perceived the upward thrust that education gave their children. They pushed and cajoled them to achieve the heights of social respectability that professional status brought, far more lasting than the mere possession of wealth. Daughters, however, did not have this dazzling perspective placed before them. Further and higher education, unless it led to the prospect of brilliant marriages, was declared a waste of time and money. The most a Jewish grammar schoolgirl in the early thirties could expect was a comfortable secretarial or Civil Service job.

The Grammar School tried its best to inculcate classical values and traditions in an alien environment. Most of us were too poor to go on the trips abroad, few of us had the cultural environment at home to benefit from musical appreciation, none of us ever visited an art gallery or a stately home or even were made aware of the rich architectural environment of the city we lived in. Home and school were two separate entities, so how could I ever appreciate the education I was getting at such cost to my parents. (I was never allowed to forget that). All the masters wore their gowns and belonged to a different world. Even those we liked were never our friends. They distrusted us, and bestowed praise grudgingly. The boy who sat in front of me, now a Reader in Applied Economics at Cambridge, received the same amount of bitchy criticism as I did.

Coming to the school from the comfortable atmosphere of the primary school, where I was always top of the class, was a shock. It was so big with cold stone corridors and huge oaken doors, ancient and gnarled furniture, dozens of teachers who came and went with a twirl of their gowns, and a host of rules that had to be obeyed. There was a subtle class and social division that soon became apparent. Firstly the division between Jews and non-Jews. Secondly, the division between fee-paying and scholarship boys and, thirdly, the gap between those who came from the south side — Clapton and those from the more prosperous north — Stamford Hill. Since I was only a Jewish scholarship boy from Clapton, I was at the bottom of the pile. I was never really motivated and along with all my friends we drifted along in the middle of the school, never achieving very much. None of my family ever set foot in my school and I doubt whether they knew the names of the schoolmasters that taught me. My world of school was kept rigidly apart from my world of home. There were no parents' evening and school activities, such as the School Concert, the School Play or the School Gym Display, certainly did not attract or interest my parents or my sister or brother.

So, in spite of its emphasis on tradition and the maintenance of values, the school had only a divisive impact on our society. It effectively separated its scholars from their contemporaries in the other — the elementary and secondary schools. Those boys I knew in the junior school, who never made it to the grammer school, I never spoke to nor saw again. But for thousands, the Grammar School did represent an escape, an escape from their environment. And so began the exodus from the inner cities, the seeds were sown then. It is ironic that the children of these grammar schoolboys have now returned to Hackney, Islington, Finsbury Park and Canonbury and set up home in the smartened up houses, terraces and flats. Presumably the cycle will continue with their children going to the schools attended by their grand-parents.

10   The Early Thirties

But what were the days like in the mid-thirties? Trams had still not been entirely superseded by the trolleybus. Trams ran under one traction in the L.C.C. (London County Council) area and changed to another outside. This led to a laborious system of bringing down a pole that was fixed to the roof which made contact with the system of overhead wires, and pushing a transformer under the tram to make contact with a third open rail that ran down the middle of the track. The overhead pole had to be caught by a clumsy long-handled hook wielded by the conductor, while another man pushed the transformer under the tram. This was a continuous job which always fascinated me as a small boy since the transfer junction was at the bottom of the road we now lived in, in Lea Bridge Road. I would often watch them. It was also just opposite a cut-price confectioners' that sold "Penny Nestles" at two for one and a half pence! I always allowed myself two a week out of my sixpence pocket money. The rest would go on buying foreign stamps or the occasional Hotspur or Wizard.

The sweet shop was a marvel of goodies. Behind the assistant were serried ranks of half pound slabs of chocolate, Terry's, Rowntrees, Nestles, Cadburys, all priced at six and a half pence instead of eightpence. It was my ambition to wait for a fortnight and buy one, a Rowntrees Extra Creamy half pound slab, but I never did. However, I can console myself that my teeth have stood me in good stead as a result of not eating very many sweets or chocolates!

Life at home was centred entirely in the kitchen. The radio was put on as soon as either my brother or sister came in, and wasn't switched off until they went to bed. My father used to grumble at the continuous jazz that was played. He hated it, especially when he wanted to read extracts from his newspaper to us. I would have to spread out my schoolbooks on the kitchen table, which was now permanently laid for a meal, and do my homework against this background of noise. I would stuff my fingers into my ears when learning a poem or some French or Latin vocabulary. I suppose I was a bit of a nuisance, taking up so much room, and shutting myself off from the others. Being the youngest, I was expected to bring in the dishes, find people's glasses, newspapers, fill up the water jugs — my father drank pints and pints of water with his meals — and so on. We had a large dresser in the kitchen with two huge copious drawers which contained almost everything, the bric-a-brac of a generation and a half, and I was constantly diving in to get something for someone.

During the day the house was quiet. The tenants' two girls were at school and only my mother and I were in for lunch. In the evenings, there was much more hustle and bustle, for everyone came in from work at different times, and ate separately. We never sat down as a family to a meal except at High Festivals. My sister worked incredibly long hours. She was a shop assistant and worked in dress shops — in the original Wallis shop among others. Selling clothes wasn't easy so shops kept open for fifteen hours for six days a week in order to make enough sales. One device these Jewish dress shops employed was to engage a man to stand outside the shop and try to entice passers-by inside. If they bought anything this man, often the only man on the staff, commonly called the "slapper", would share in the commission on the sale. So my sister had little time for social activity and therefore less opportunity for finding a marriage partner, especially as she had a Sunday morning job.

So my sister never ate with us, and when my brother came home, usually pretty tired after long exhausting hours in the furniture factory, he would spread his newspaper on the table, put his plate of food on it, and read around his plate whilst he ate. As soon as he finished he would change and go out to see his friends. They were never invited to our house and he never spoke about his life at work or after work. No one ever asked him either. As the radio had been switched on by him, it stayed on. I went to bed comparatively early. There was a strict rule in our house that children had to be in bed before their parents, and as my mother always went to bed by 10 p.m., I had to go fairly early. What was annoying was being woken almost every night by my brother when he came home and climbed into our bed.

11 The Politics of the East End

The Spanish Civil War was a landmark in my life. I wished I was old enough to join the International Brigade and I knew one or two men who were going off to fight for Republican Spain. I held a simplistic view of politics. The Jews had to be defended at all costs, therefore Hitler was evil and should be stopped. I was very distressed at the stories that were coming out of Germany, at the persecution of the Jews, and I longed to be able to do something myself. The local Communists were organising anti-Fascist rallies, and clashes were growing more frequent.

One of my friends and I would go to a market place, Ridley Road in Dalston, where the Independent Labour Party, Communist Party and British Union of Fascists would compete to get command of the rostrum. The secret was to get a few youngsters to hang around early in the day where the platform was to be erected, and as soon as the market stalls were packing up, to stand on the spot where the platform was to be fixed and the meeting to be held. It was pretty terrifying for me and a few other Jewish lads to be facing the Fascist thugs and bully boys who tried to edge us out and claim the pitch for themselves. Later, the police put a stop to this practice. Both sides held their meetings simultaneously and as the tension grew so did the clashes and violence. Then ultimately came the ban on all marches and processions. We were involved, nevertheless, in some ugly scenes with local Blackshirts and I suffered much personal anti-semitic abuse. My mother, confined tightly to her narrow Jewish circle of shops and friends, shielded herself against this, but I could never understand why my brother and father were so passive. In the end I was told to keep out of it and my drift towards the Young Communist League was halted. I wasn't allowed to bring any literature home and I had to stop seeing my political friends.

For the Jews were in a dilemma. Many of them had entered public life, were part of the establishment, and yet others, like my parents, felt they were still visitors. They had to keep quiet in order to stay. What they were haunted with was the memory of the pogroms in Eastern Europe. They had seen a German Jewish community, once so strong and wealthy, annihilated and, if it could happen there could it not happen here in England which seemed so much more hostile and less friendly than Germany had been? So the preachers in the synagogues condemned the actions of the Nazis in the fullest possible terms yet ordered Jews not to be provocative. The fact that ome of the leading Communists and Socialists were Jews was a matter of regret, not pride. And so I was told to "stop messing about with politics, you are too young to understand" and, to my shame, I acquiesced.

The two girls that lived in our house worried me. They were the first girls I had any contact with, but they kept very much to themselves, and although we lived together in the same house for five years, I only spoke to them outside the presence of their mother about three or four times. My mother was very strict and conventional about matters of sex. She instilled in me a belief that Jewish girls did not flirt and did not encourage boys to make overtures. Actually most of the girls I met from then on, and they all had to be Jewish, behaved exactly like that. Cold, aloof and immensely superior. How could I reconcile this with the chatting up that occurred outside synagogues on High Festivals. So nice Jewish girls, one of whom would become my wife, were put on a pedestal and stayed there for years. This again was part of the Jewish ethos, to maintain some kind of moral superiority and to justify the title "The Chosen People". Every Jewish mother wanted her son to marry a "nice Jewish girl" and so only non-Jewish girls indulged in necking and petting and only the not so nice Jewish boys went out with non-Jewish girls. I certainly was a naive young man and so were all my friends. It was some years before I indulged in the, at first, hesitant and later more confident groping and touching of bodies and exploring the joys of sexual contact. I suppose most of the girls I met during those years must have been told the same things by their mothers. Certainly none of them made the slightest overture or maybe I just put them off by my earnestness.

So we went around in a large group, rather noisy and boister-ous, and very very clannish. None of us had much money so our pleasures were very simple. The occasional visit to the cinema for fivepence when we were able to persuade someone to take us in, spending many hours in the park or playing fields or visiting one another's houses. My middle class children followed an entirely different pattern, aided by the family car and only a small circle of friends, but enjoying a large number of family outings and holidays.

My friends and I were left to our own devices. We would spend hours in the local stamp dealer's shop in Upper Clapton Road whilst the fortunate one or two who had any money to spend chose some stamps aided by us. We walked everywhere, to the parks, the library, the baths and this spun out the time we would spend together. Going to Springfield Park was a popular pastime. It had space and freedom. I must have known every blade of grass. We watched the men playing bowls, the girls playing tennis and the boys rowing on the River Lea. Strangely enough, my future wife was walking through the park at the same time, though I wouldn't have given a second glance to this little girl, seven years younger than me.

We followed the fortunes of Jack Hobbs — everyone's hero — and Sutcliffe, of Verity and Larwood, and of Joey Hulme and Boy Bastin. Sport attracted a large following, very orderly and with much good humour. Clapton Orient was our local football club but, to our disgust, they deserted us and moved to Leyton. We had a week-long debate in school on the disastrous effect of this move. For some reason which I shall never know, Jewish boys tended to support Tottenham Hotspur though we never got the religious division in support for football clubs as was the case in Glasgow. It was just as well, for racial tension was high enough without introducing it into this dimension.

12   My Father

My father took me to the factory where he worked off Albion Road
during the summer of 1937. I suppose he wanted to see how I
would cope as a cabinet maker should I leave school. He should
have been forewarned by my progress in woodworking classes at
school. I had never got beyond the first exercise. On our arrival in
the woodworking centre, the instructor, a large sarcastic bully,
who hated Jews, gave us a lecture on the use of tools; he then
flung at us all a large chunk of rough wood and asked us to plane
it into a perfect oblong. So I set to with a plane and a T-square and
tried to plane it to a smooth level piece of wood. The shavings
around me grew, the wood got thinner and thinner, until it, still
sloping and obviously far from level, became unplaneable. I suffered the ignominy of showing this miserable shaving to the ogre
or his assistance, who was almost as bad. Another piece of wood
was flung at me and I returned to my plane, my pile of shavings,
and the impossible task of getting the wretched thing planed
square. So I planed away throughout the term and then throughout the year, while everyone around me was making teapot
stands, plate racks, clocks, pencil cases and even dolls' houses.
Never a word was exchanged between the master and me. He
held me in complete and utter contempt, and I struggled with the
humiliation of it all. The following year, which was to be my last,
I was asked to do a mortice joint. I was very good at drawing the
plan on the piece of wood, but my efforts with hammer and chisel
were equally disastrous. Perhaps I was marginally better with a
chisel and hammer than with a plane, but I still spent the whole
year destroying pieces of wood in the attempt to make a mortice
joint. I was advised by the woodwork master, and I took his advice
most eagerly, that I should drop woodwork. I was quite the worst
he had ever seen. So, I thought I had turned my back on such
heart-breaking tasks.

Years later when we were first married, Renee asked me to
fix a small hook in the kitchen for a tea towel. I surveyed the
scene, decided that I hadn't the right tools for such a technical job,
and went out to buy a Rawlplug outfit. As far as I was concerned,
power drills hadn't been invented. To use the Rawlplug outfit, one
had to hammer a heavy piece of metal into the wall, to create a
hole which was the correct size for the Rawlplug. I swung at this
tool with a hammer and immediately a shower of plaster came

raining down on our newly decorated kitchen, and a huge hole appeared in the wall. The boy who lived in the room on the other side of the wall came rushing in. Luckily I stopped. One more swing, and I would probably have gone through into his bedroom. My wife said not a word but set about clearing up the mess. We covered the hole with a calendar and hung the tea cloth over the edge of the cooker. Clearly, I was not what one would call a practical man.

So when my father organised a place for me to work during the summer holidays, I couldn't imagine what I could do, but the eight shillings a week pocket money seemed a small fortune to me. Eight shillings for seven weeks would give me a lot of money indeed. As I travelled with my father to work I realised how little I had known him. I had seen him bantering and baiting my mother, watched him playing with my niece and listening to the stories he told her, which were always the same and concerned a fierce bear in a thick forest. But now I felt quite manly striding along with him, with a packet of thick sandwiches in my hand. I suppose I began to appreciate the qualities of my father for the very first time in my life.

He was a short tough wiry man with a very bristly moustache. All his life he had worked long hours on hard physical application of his skills, acquired without any formal training. I don't suppose there had been any kind of apprenticeship training in Czarist Russia and since he had been called up to serve in the Army at the age of 20, most of his working life was spent firstly in the sweatshops of England at the beginning of the century and then in the small cramped workshops in London's East End until the end of the thirties when he moved as a worker to one of the newer industrial units in north London. He was to end his working life back in one of those disreputable ramshackle workshops after the War with my brother. This last fling at being a master cabinet maker ended in complete failure, my father finally, after four years, retiring for good and my brother emigrating to the U.S.A. to meet up with his cousins in New York to complete symbolically the journey my father began fifty years previously.

He and my mother were such poles apart in temperament. She was glum, pessimistic, narrow in outlook and obsessed with domestic chores. Perpetually short of money she grumbled at the slightest hint of extravagance. Her own life was frugal, she ate

"Cyril's Mother and Father".

the leftovers from yesterday's meals and would often be satisfied with a bare slice of bread. My father, however, longed to live on a grander scale. He should have married a woman with drive and ambition who would spur him on, guide him in financial management and develop his abilities. He was everybody's friend, and I never met anyone who said a bad word against him. Amongst his circle he was known as "The Professor" though I realised early on that his knowledge was fairly superficial. At least amongst his contemporaries he was head and shoulders above them in intellect and he would win every argument. His only drawback was a fiery temper, mellowed as the years passed, but if crossed in argument he would shout and bang the table, shaming my mother.

Altogether a too generous man, he gave away much of his hard earned money to support friends and colleagues who came to him for help. He was the sort of man who would buy three rounds of drinks for every other person's one and people probably traded on his generosity. I knew him but little as a child, just as the awe-inspiring parent who led me off to synagogue or who told me and my niece the occasional story. I really remember him best in his later years when he would terrify us all by the way he charged across roads. He never came to terms with the increased traffic in London, refused to recognise that cars were dangerous and lorries and buses even more so, and would simply walk off the pavement and straight across the road in the face of on coming traffic. In his last few years he nursed my mother, learned to do the shopping, but died some years before her, rather quickly and suddenly, with a lifetime of ambitions and desires unfulfilled.

In 1937 I was working alongside him in Turner's furniture factory just off Albion Road. My job consisted of making tea, running off to the coffee shop for sandwiches, cigarettes, cakes, helping to move large pieces of furniture around, and sandpapering any rough edges on beds and cupboards. Sandpapering was the nearest I ever got to a technical job and, like my planing activities at school, the job was endless and utterly and thoroughly boring. It was agreed by all the family at the end of that period that I would never become a cabinet maker.

Thence followed the second family discussion about my future. My brother and sister felt that I should leave school as I was now 15. My father was in two minds about it, I think he was secretly pleased that I had got into the grammar school, though he never expressed it. He needed the additional money I would bring in. My mother, as usual, said nothing. My eldest sister, who could be quite a firebrand, laid into them. The job prospects that were dangled in front of me were taxi-driving and hairdressing. These were regarded as fairly respectable jobs among Jews, since they could lead to one becoming self-employed, and had the advantage of being a trade. To me both suggestions seemed positively ludicrous, and in the end my sister won, and I was allowed to stay on at school for one more year to take the School Certificate examination.

13   Leaving School

I knew war would break out. I followed the fortunes of Republican Spain and grew more and more angry at the Government's non-intervention policy. I joined in the activities of the Popular Front and was brought into close contact with members of the British Communist Party. I went to meetings where members of the International Brigade spoke of life on the front in Spain. That this was the rehearsal for the war in Europe was absolutely certain. If I had been old enough, I would have joined the Communist Party — the Young Communist League never attracted me — but I stayed on the edge as a sympathiser. None of my friends were all that politically motivated though we were all united in our hatred of Hitler and his obscene anti-semitic policy. Spain was the most emotive experience of my life and overshadowed my work at school. Consequently I did worse than expected, failing to get the important Matriculation examination, though gaining the School Certificate with four credits.

So there I was in July 1938, the year of Munich and further appeasement, with a School Certificate. My friends who had matriculated were either going on to take the Civil Service entrance examinations or moving into some respectable Local Government job, or even contemplating Higher School Certificate and the Sixth Form. Our school had three Sixth Forms. The Science Sixth where all the potential doctors were going, the Arts Sixth which was mainly for those embarking on a legal career, and the rest, lumped together in the Commercial Sixth. About 80% of the boys staying on were Jewish, and almost all destined to become doctors, dentists, lawyers and solicitors. Philosophy, languages, mathematics, and similar subjects only led to teaching, and no-one wanted to enter such an underpaid and unprivileged profession. Finding a job proved very difficult being a rather podgy youth with only an average academic record I tried without success for dozens of fairly humdrum clerical jobs. One incident still remains vividly in my mind. I had replied to an advertisement for a junior clerk in a small engineering firm in Walthamstow. After a couple of weeks I received a letter asking me to attend for interview. I went along hopefully and presented myself at the enquiry desk, where a young man told me to wait. About ten minutes later he came back, bobbing and grimacing in front of me, to tell me the job had been filled. I knew instinctively that I had lost the job because I was a Jew. For the first time in my life hatred welled up in me and I wanted to punch that bobbing dancing face in front of me. I needed that job.

Eventually I got a job as a clerk with a firm of New York jobbers bearing the delightful name of Post and Flagg. A lot of the staff came in at noon and worked until 8 or 9 p.m. when the New York Stock Exchange closed. I, however, worked normal hours and one of my jobs was to take documents, cheques, promissory notes, to various financial institutions in the City. I was provided with a huge thick black waterproof to protect me in the winter and the document bag which was strapped to my wrist. All over the City in those days were street sellers displaying large numbers of chocolate bars. Wherever one went one would find on a corner an enormous selection of twopenny chocolate bars. Competition was very keen among chocolate manufacturers who were bringing out new bars almost every week, and my mouth would literally water as I gazed on these delightful displays. Alas, I couldn't afford to buy any. I earned 22/6d per week, gave my mother 15/- and the rest was for fares and clothes. So a bar of chocolate was a rare luxury indeed. Still they did help to brighten up the rather drab alleyways of the City of London.

In January 1939, the London office of Post and Flagg was closed. I had received three weeks' warning of closure and two weeks notice, so once again I was looking for a job at a time when the political scene was worsening. I took the very first job that was offered me, in the Walks Dept. of H. Samuel & Co. Ltd., merchant bankers. The Walks Department was the grandiose name for messengers. We were all young ex-grammar schoolboys who took this job as a way into banking. Once employed we could work for the Institute of Bankers examinations and get transferred to another department. I learned the geography of the City of London even more as I trudge around taking and delivering documents from the various financial institutions. For this excruciatingly boring job I received 25/- a week and a bar of Pears soap and a posh towel to use in the staff lavatories. The soap was a real perk. They lasted for most of the war in my mother's house even though I only worked for eighteen months with H. Samuel & Co. Ltd. We helped the Post Department in the afternoons when our walking was done — documents and money could only be transferred during banking hours, and we provided the only element of hilarity in the august, sombre and very respectable banking hall where no one spoke much above a whisper. Often we were admonished for our noise and general disposition, but it did make life bearable. To my family and friends and neighbours I had a very respectable job. I worked in a Bank, in the City, dressed in a suit with a small suitcase to carry my lunch, and I bought my own copy of the News Chronicle. No one ever asked me about my job, or what I did, which was just as well. In any case I was going to enroll in September for an evening course for the Bankers examinations.

That was never to be. In September we were at War, and no one thought about evening classes. Why, we might be dead in a week! I was under no illusions about the military strength of Germany. For years I had seen displays of their military power, the ease with which they had overpowered Austria and Czechoslovakia, and I was convinced they would make a devastating attack on us. Of course, they should have but to our relief and for the future peace of the world, they did not.

The Russo-German non-aggression pact stunned me and my flirtation with the Communist Party ended. I hated Hitler and all that he stood for, was glad that Chamberlain had been pushed into war at last and I could not accept that Communist call to oppose the War. I still had a sympathy for those neighbours and friends who had gone to fight in Spain, and felt that they had been badly let down by the Ribbentrop-Molotov Pact.

My family, of course, were panicking. They rushed off into the air-raid shelter in the garden when the first, and false, air raid siren sounded on Sunday, September 3rd, soon after Chamberlain had declared on the radio that we were at war with Germany. We pasted brown sticky tape on the windows, fixed blackout curtains and waited for the Germans to come. My mother was terrified, her mind, no doubt, going back forty years to the Pogroms of Czarist Russia. My eldest sister Eva was almost hysterical, but, as she had a young child, Vivienne, was immediately evacuated whilst her eldest daughter, Lilyan, aged 12, was evacuated in the opposite direction with her school. Thus families were split up in those hectic, terrorised days, and morale was low. That would have been the time for Hitler's blitzkrieg, but he waited, and we waited, and so dawned those strange months of the phoney war, when nothing happened and we sang "Run Rabbit Run" and "We're going to Hang Out Our Washing on the

Siegfried Line". We cared no more for Poland than we did for Czechoslovakia, though we had gone to war over Poland and slowly we relaxed a little and followed a fairly strange life which was no different from our neighbours.

Panic in the home subsided a bit. My brother and his recently married wife went off to live in Hertfordshire where he got a job working on Mosquito aircraft. Half the staff at the bank moved to a stately home in Banbury, Oxfordshire whilst the remainder of us, minus those that had joined H.M. Forces, carried on as normal or as near normal as possible. A more informal atmosphere developed and the camaraderie of a nation at war spread.

In the Spring the blitzkrieg was on and events followed in shattering sequence. The debacle of Norway, the loss of the Low Countries, the collapse of France, the bundling out of Chamberlain and the retreat from Dunkirk swept us on, leaving us in the glorious early summer of 1940 entirely on our own, or so it seemed, to face the Germans. The rest is history. For me, too, life changed. By the end of that year I was in the R.A.F. and life for me would never be the same. I had left the tight, cosy, little Jewish family environment for ever. The Jewish boy grew up and that old East End world disappeared. This book ends rather suddenly. My childhood and adolescent years ended rather suddenly — 1940 was a dramatic year for all of us, least of all myself. That is how I want to portray it. There may be a further story for me to write, but it is not Volla Volla Jew Boy.

What can we learn of these times? Most of the Jews have gone from the areas I have described, taking with them their shops, synagogues, factories and culture. Immigrants from Asia and the West Indies have come, bringing a new culture and a new vitality to the streets of Hackney. What will the young men and women growing up now say to their children in fifty years time and what will be happening in the streets of East London then? It does seem that history is repeating itself and my life and feelings are repeated in the lives and feelings of many Asian and Afro-Caribbean young men and women. We take from existing cultures, but we give something back to it.

If you enjoyed this book you might like to know about the other
books which Centerprise have published.
You can obtain a catalogue by sending a S.A.E. to

The Publishing Project
Centerprise
136/138 Kingland High St.
Hackney
London E8 2NS